Usborne

My First
COMPUTER
CODING BOOK

using

Rosie Dickins

Illustrated by Shaw Nielsen and Pete Taylor

Designed by Freya Harrison

Computer consultant: Ben Woodhall

CONTENTS

ABOUT THIS BOOK

This book is an absolute beginner's guide to computers and coding ('coding' means creating instructions for computers).

Read on to discover how computers work, then learn how to code by making your own animated characters, stories and games.

If you want to find out even MORE about computers and coding, go to:

www.usborne.com/quicklinks

and type in the keywords 'ScratchJr'. *

* Usborne Publishing is not responsible for the content of any website other than its own. Please see page 47 for advice on using the internet safely.

MEET THE COMPUTERS

A computer is a kind of machine.
It can follow instructions and work things out.

I can do lots of
different things.

Computer

VS

This always does the
same thing.

NOT a computer

Computers come in different shapes and sizes.

This is a laptop computer.

This is a tablet computer.

This is a smartphone.

It has a folding screen
and a keyboard.

You tell it what to do
by touching the screen.

This is a tiny computer
and telephone combined.

TAKE A CLOSER LOOK

Here's a tablet up close. The little square pictures, known as **icons**, show different things it can do.

Different tablets and icons will look slightly different, but do most of the same things.

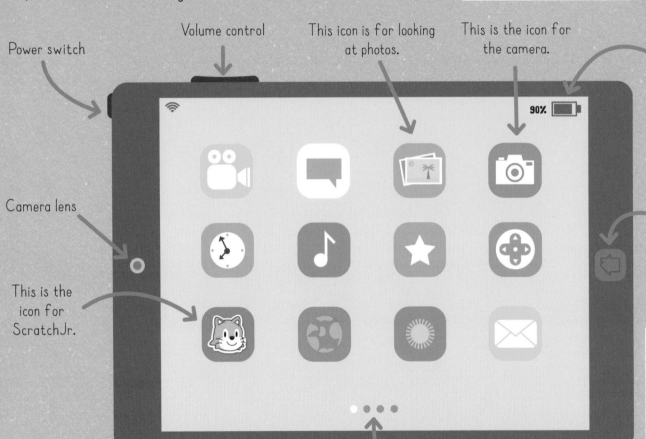

Volume control

Power switch

This icon is for looking at photos.

This is the icon for the camera.

90%

Battery symbol
This shows how much power is left. When it gets low, the tablet must be plugged in to charge.

Camera lens

Home button
On some tablets, this is a picture of a house on the screen.

This is the icon for ScratchJr.

If the screen is dark, press the home button or power switch to wake it up.

Each icon represents a program or **app** stored on the tablet.

Each of these dots represents a screenful or **page** of icons. Swipe left or right to change the page.

WHAT'S INSIDE?

Most computers have similar parts inside. For example, if you took apart the tablet on the left you'd see...

WARNING!

DON'T try taking a computer apart yourself. The parts are fragile and some could be dangerous if handled in the wrong way.

SCREEN
This has a layer of tiny dots or **pixels** which light up to make pictures.

CAMERA
This camera faces the front. There is another camera facing the back.

BATTERY
This stores electrical power.

CASE
This protects the insides.

GLASS
This protects the screen. It also has sensors which can tell when you touch it.

CIRCUIT BOARD
This holds the **chips** – little blocks which are the computer's 'brains'.

REMEMBER

It's dangerous to mix electricity and water – so never let a computer get wet!

CONNECTORS
These let the tablet 'talk' to other devices.

SPEAKERS
These play sounds.

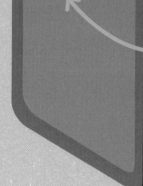

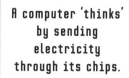

A computer 'thinks' by sending electricity through its chips.

7

HOW DOES IT WORK?

To make all the bits and pieces inside the tablet work, you need the right instructions. That's where **apps** come in...

AMAZING APPS

An app is a set of instructions for a particular task. You don't usually *see* the instructions, only what happens as a result.

For example, if you use the camera app to take a photo...

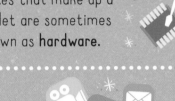

The solid bits and pieces that make up a tablet are sometimes known as **hardware**.

The instructions or apps that control them are known as **software**.

Take photo!

MEANWHILE INSIDE THE TABLET...

Oof!

Notice button press

Store picture from camera

Freeze picture on screen

Click!

Make 'click' sound

Send stored picture to 'Photos'

Unfreeze picture on screen

In computer terms, this is described as turning *input* into *output*...

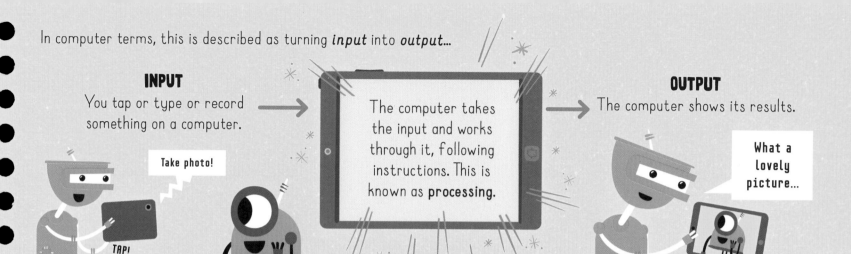

INPUT
You tap or type or record something on a computer.

Take photo!

TAP!

The computer takes the input and works through it, following instructions. This is known as **processing**.

OUTPUT
The computer shows its results.

What a lovely picture...

USING APPS

Before you can use an app, you need to open it.

To open an app, tap its icon and the screen will change to show the app.

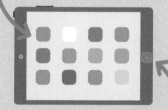

To go back to the screen with the icons, press the home button.

Sometimes, several apps are stored together inside a **folder**.

My games

Tap the folder to open it and see the apps inside...

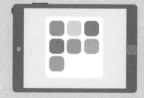

To close the folder again, press the home button.

FINDING THINGS

If you can't see the app you want, you can use the **search box** to find it.

Tap the box and a keyboard will pop up. Type the name of the app, then tap 'search'.

🔍 Search

If the search box isn't showing, swipe right until it appears.

CODING

Writing instructions for a computer is known as coding.
Anyone can do it – but you have to know how.

COMPUTERS AREN'T SMART

Computers can only follow very clear, exact instructions. They will follow the instructions *exactly*, even if the instructions are wrong. For example...

COME IN!

KNOCK KNOCK!

OH NO, I FORGOT TO SAY OPEN THE DOOR!

WARNING!

Computers can't think for themselves or use common sense – they don't have any!

On the plus side, computers are very good at long, complicated tasks, because they don't get bored or forget things.

12,120 + 35,001 x 42 - 16,495 + 2,658 ÷ 5

393,849

Computers are incredibly fast, too. An ordinary tablet can do millions of calculations every second. And if you can code, that power is at your fingertips.

CODING IS LIKE COOKING

Computer code needs to be built up in a clear, step-by-step way. It's similar to a recipe. If you put the steps in the wrong order, or if a step is missing, the recipe won't work.

BANANA SMOOTHIE

1. peel banana
2. chop banana
3. add milk
4. blend until smooth

Things that computers CAN do...

Follow commands

PEEL! **CHOP!**

Answer a yes/no question

Is it lumpy?

Yes
Keep blending.

No
Finish.

Repeat something again... and again... and again... This is known as a LOOP.

If you follow the right steps, in the right order, you should always get the same result.

In computing, a 'recipe' is known as an **algorithm**.

USING SCRATCHJR

Writing code might sound tricky, but there are apps designed to help. This book will show you how to use an app called ScratchJr.

ScratchJr makes coding easier by giving you lots of ready-made instructions, which snap together like jigsaw pieces.

With ScratchJr, you can create characters and scenes, and bring them to life. The shapes of the pieces will help you get things in the right order.

ScratchJr runs on most tablets and you can download it for free. If you don't have it already, go to

www.usborne.com/quicklinks

for a link and full instructions.

FIRST STEPS

The next pages will show you how to get started
with ScratchJr and make a character move.

Find the cat icon on the home screen. Tap on it to open ScratchJr. Then...

1. Tap on the house to open
the **project page**.

2. Tap on the **plus sign** to
start a new project.

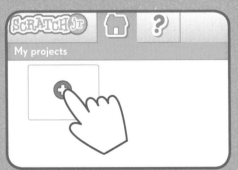

3. Every new project begins like this.

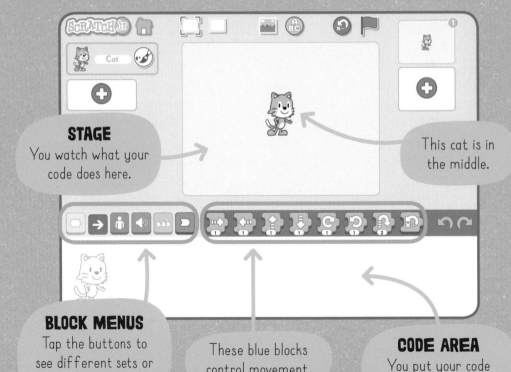

STAGE
You watch what your
code does here.

This cat is in
the middle.

BLOCK MENUS
Tap the buttons to
see different sets or
'menus' of blocks.

These blue blocks
control movement.

CODE AREA
You put your code
together here.

MAKE A MOVE

Code area

1. Drag the first blue block into the code area, and let go. Tap it. The cat on stage should move to the right.

Reset button

2. Tap a few more times. The cat should move each time. Tap the reset button to send it back to the start.

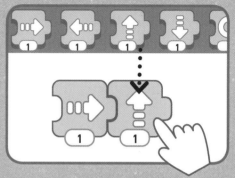

3. Drag another block beside the first. When you let go, the two blocks should snap together.

To move further, tap the number and enter a bigger number.

4. Tap either block to play your code. Blocks always play from left to right, lighting up as they play.

5. The cat will move the way the arrows point. If it goes off one side of the stage, it will reappear on the other.

Congratulations, you've made your first piece of code!

MORE MOVES

1. Try adding more blocks, and moving blocks around. (There are some tips on moving blocks on the right.)

Can you make the cat jump and spin around?

This makes the cat spin.

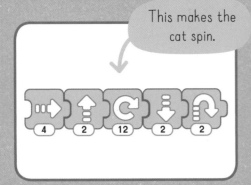

2. The blocks we used are shown above, but you could use any combination you like. Tap any block to play the whole line, or 'script'.

*A finished line of blocks is known as a **script**.*

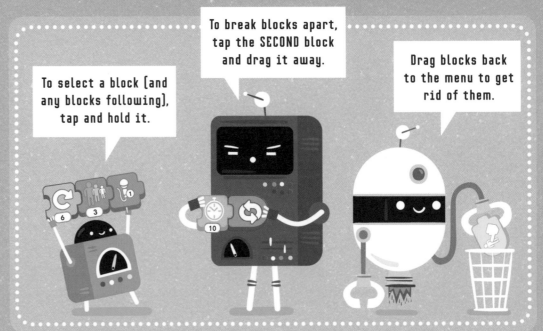

To select a block (and any blocks following), tap and hold it.

To break blocks apart, tap the SECOND block and drag it away.

Drag blocks back to the menu to get rid of them.

FINISHING

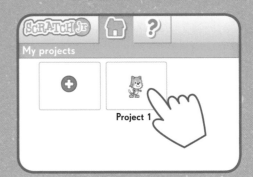

1. When you're finished, tap the house at the top of the screen. This takes you back to the project page.

2. Your cat project will be numbered and saved automatically. You can go back to it by tapping its picture. (See page 42 if you want to name it.)

BUTTONS AND BLOCKS

Here is a guide to the buttons around the stage.

ScratchJr has six **block menus**, each with its own color. Tap a menu button to see that set of blocks.

 Yellow 'trigger' menu.
These blocks control how a script begins – for example, when you tap something.

 Blue 'motion' menu.
These blocks make characters move.

 Purple 'looks' menu.
These blocks control how characters look. You can make them change size or even disappear.

 Green 'sound' menu.
These blocks let you record and play sounds.

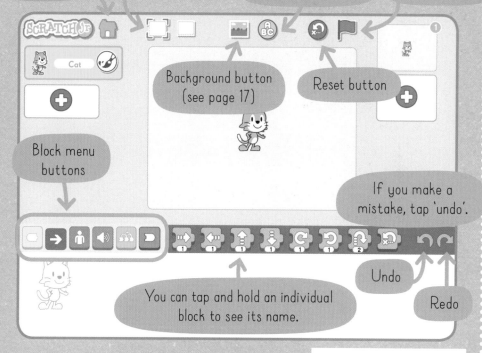

Project page button

Full-screen button (see page 18)

Button for adding text (see page 29)

Green flag

Background button (see page 17)

Reset button

Block menu buttons

If you make a mistake, tap 'undo'.

You can tap and hold an individual block to see its name.

Undo

Redo

 Orange 'control' menu.
These blocks control other blocks – for example, how often or how fast they are played.

 Red 'end' menu.
These blocks control what happens at the end of a script, making it repeat or stop completely.

Read on to discover how to use different kinds of blocks.

NOISY FARM

Find out how to record your own sounds and create a noisy farm, using sound blocks.

Start a new project by tapping the plus sign on the project page. Then...

REPLACE THE CAT

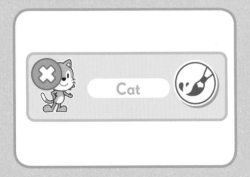

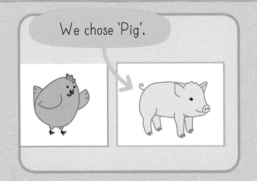

We chose 'Pig'.

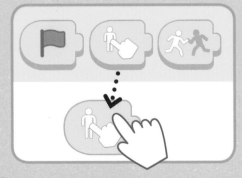

1. Tap and hold the little cat on the left, until a red 'X appears. Then tap the X to delete the cat.

2. Tap the plus sign on the left, to bring up a list of characters. Tap to select one. Tap again to add it to the stage.

3. Tap the yellow block to see the yellow 'trigger' menu. Drag this 'start on touch' block to your coding area.

MORNING

MEH

MOOO

ADD A SOUND

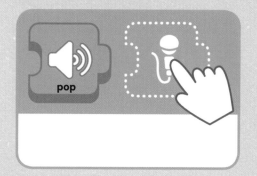

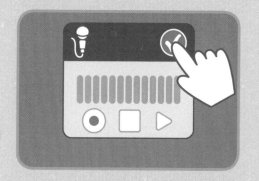

1. Tap the green block to see the green 'sounds' menu. Then tap the microphone block outline, and you will get a set of recording buttons.

2. Tap the red circle and make an animal noise. Tap the square to stop recording. Tap the triangle to play your noise.

3. If you want to redo your noise, tap the circle again. Otherwise, tap the check mark to finish. You should now see a new microphone block in the sounds menu.

SET THE SCENE

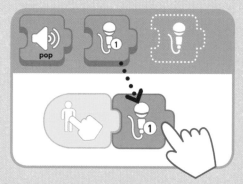

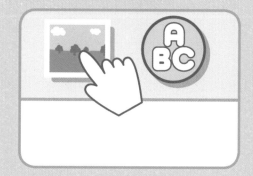

4. Drag the new block to join your 'start on touch' block. Now touch the pig on stage. It should make a noise!

1. Tap the background button above the stage. This brings up a list of backgrounds.

2. Find one you like and tap to select it. Tap again (or tap the check mark at the top) to make it appear on the stage.

ADD MORE ANIMALS

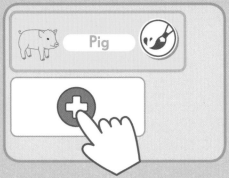

1. Tap the blue plus sign to see the character list. Find one you like and tap twice to add it to the stage.

2. Drag it into position. Then give it its own yellow 'start on touch' block and record a new noise for it, as before.

3. You can add as many characters as you like. Try adding a few, giving each one its own noise.

KEEPING TRACK

You can only see the scripts for one character at a time. To switch, tap the little character pictures on the left.

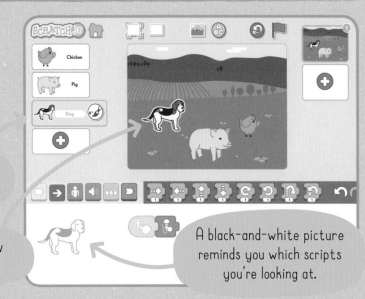

Your current character is marked in orange...

...and has a white glow around it on stage.

A black-and-white picture reminds you which scripts you're looking at.

GO LARGE

To make the stage fill the screen, tap the 'full screen' button at the top.

To return to the coding screen, tap the 'shrink' button in the top left corner.

DRIVING ALONG

Find out how to change speeds and create
a road scene with moving traffic.

Start a new project by tapping the plus sign on the project page. Then...

PUT A CAR ON A ROAD

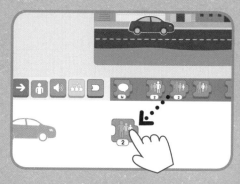

1. Tap and hold the cat, and tap the X to delete it. Tap the plus sign to see the character list. Scroll down to 'Car' and tap twice to add it.

2. Tap the background button. Find one you like (we chose 'City') and tap twice to make it appear on the stage. Now, the car seems too big...

3. Tap the purple block for the 'looks' menu. Drag out a 'shrink' block and tap it a few times. Then drag the shrunk car to where you want it.

HONK!

TURN THE PAGE TO MAKE THE CAR DRIVE, AND ADD MORE TRAFFIC.

DRIVE ALONG

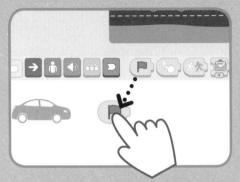

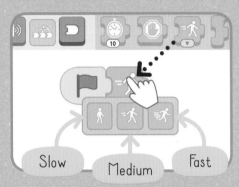

1. Open the yellow 'trigger' menu. Drag out a 'start on green flag' block. (This will make the script start if you tap the **green flag** above the stage.)

2. Open the orange 'control' menu and add a 'speed' block. Tap the arrow on the block to pick **which** speed.

3. Open the blue 'motion' menu. Add a 'move right' block, tap the number and make it 20. Then tap the green flag above the stage and watch...

MORE TRAFFIC

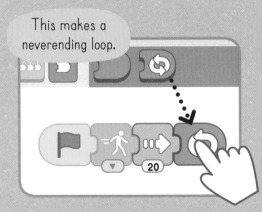

This makes a neverending loop.

4. If you want to make the car **keep** going, go to the red 'end' menu and add a 'repeat forever' block.

1. Tap the plus sign on the left to add new characters. Add another car and a bus. Shrink and drag them into place.

2. To change the new car's color, tap the paintbrush. This takes you to a screen where you can paint it.

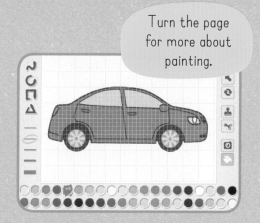

3. Tap the paint can. Choose a color, then tap the car to fill it in. Tap the check mark to finish and return to the stage.

4. You can copy your original script by dragging it from the coding area to each of your new characters.

5. Now if you tap the new car or bus, you should see the same script. Tap the arrow on the 'speed' block to set the speed.

HONK HONK

1. With the new car highlighted, open the green 'sounds' menu. Tap the microphone and record a 'honk'.

2. Drag out your new 'sounds' block and add a 'start on touch'. Now touch the new car on stage. It should honk.

WEE-OOH!

VROOM!

Try giving each character its own noise.

BEEP!

PAINTING THINGS

ScratchJr has a painting screen where you can create your own characters and backgrounds, or paint over existing ones.

If you tap a **paintbrush**, it will open a **painting screen** like this...

The little pictures around the edge show the tools you can use.

Tap here to undo whatever you did last...

...and here to redo it.

Tap the check mark to finish and save your painting.

Circle tool – draws circles and ovals.

Line tool – draws lines.

Turn tool – turns things.

Move tool – moves things.

Triangle tool – draws triangles.

Rectangle tool – draws rectangles.

Scissor tool – removes things.

Copy tool – copies things.

Tap here to pick the thickness of your brush.

The grid area is where you can paint.

Camera tool – adds photos.

Fill tool – fills an area with one tap.

Character

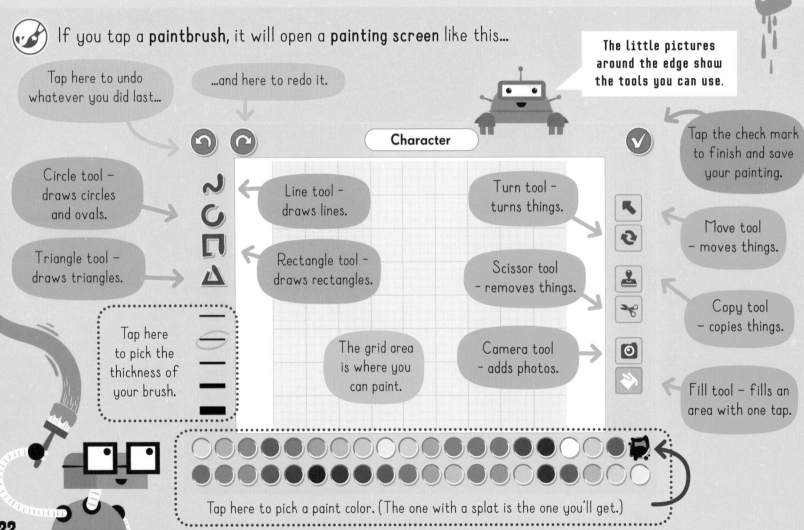

Tap here to pick a paint color. (The one with a splat is the one you'll get.)

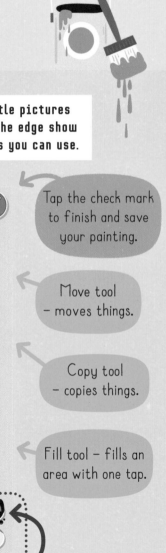

CREATE A CHARACTER

Here, you can use the painting screen to create a funny face – then bring it to life on the next page.
Start a new project and delete the cat. Then...

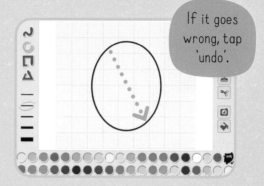

If it goes wrong, tap 'undo'.

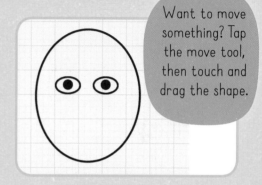

Want to move something? Tap the move tool, then touch and drag the shape.

1. Tap the plus to open the character list. Tap to select the empty box, then tap the paintbrush above it.

2. Tap the circle tool. Then drag your finger down and across the screen to make an oval face shape.

3. Add two small ovals for eyes, like this. Then tap once inside each eye, to make a dot in the middle.

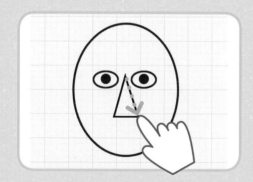

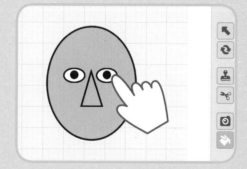

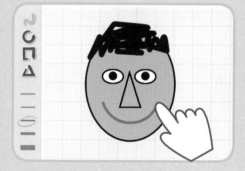

4. Now tap on the triangle tool. Starting between the eyes, drag your finger down and across to make a nose shape.

5. Tap on the fill tool and a skin color, then tap on the face to fill it in. Change to white and tap the whites of the eyes.

6. Tap the thickest brush, pick a color and draw the hair. Then tap a thinner brush, pick a color and add a mouth. Tap the check mark to finish.

WAGGLY EYEBROWS

Now for the eyebrows. To make them waggle, they need to be created as a separate character.

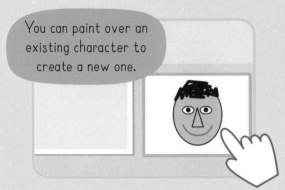

You can paint over an existing character to create a new one.

1. Tap the plus to see the character list. Tap the face you just made, then tap the paintbrush to get a copy of it in the painting screen.

2. Pick a color and use the line tool to draw two eyebrows. Change to the scissor tool, and tap all the *other* parts of the face to remove them.

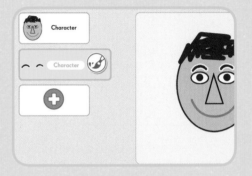

3. Tap the check mark to finish. The eyebrows will appear on the stage – highlighted in white on top of the original face – and listed as a separate character.

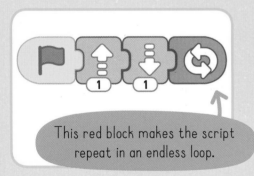

This red block makes the script repeat in an endless loop.

4. Make sure the eyebrows are highlighted in the character list. Then build the script above to waggle them up and down.

5. To test your code, tap the 'full screen' button at the top (this removes the white highlight from the eyebrows). Then tap the green flag.

When characters overlap, the last one you moved goes in front. So if you drag the face, the eyebrows will vanish! Fix this by dragging them in the right order.

PAINTING BACKGROUNDS

You can paint backgrounds in exactly the same way.

1. Tap the landscape button to open the background list. Select the empty box and tap the paintbrush.

2. Fill the screen with a sky color. Then paint a scene on top, and tap the check mark to finish. Your background will appear on stage, and in the background list.

The clouds are overlapping ovals.

To repeat a shape, tap the copy tool and then the shape.

Then drag the new copy to where you want it.

This tree is a triangle on top of a rectangle.

The ground is one big rectangle.

It's best to fill in the background first, as the fill tool doesn't work so well once there are lots of shapes.

CHANGING A BACKGROUND

1. To *change* a background, open the background list and select the one you want to alter. Then tap the paintbrush.

2. Paint over the scene, or remove parts, then tap the check mark to finish. Your new version will appear on stage, and in the background list, along with the original.

USING PHOTOS

When painting a new character, you can use photos to fill in shapes.

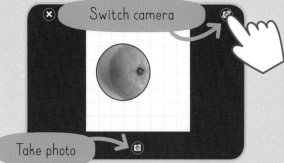

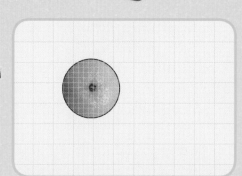

1. Draw the shape you want to fill. Tap the photo tool, then tap inside your shape. The camera starts facing you.

2. To take a photo of something in front of you, tap the 'Switch camera' button at the top.

3. Line up the picture, then tap 'Take photo'. Your photo will now appear in the painting screen.

Some of the ready-made characters have space for you to add your own photo.

1. Open the character list. Find a character with a blank face. Tap it, then tap the paintbrush.

2. Tap the photo tool, then tap inside the blank face. Move your tablet until you see your face there.

3. Tap the 'Take photo' button. Then tap the check mark to finish and see yourself on stage.

BIRTHDAY CAKE

Discover how to use looks blocks to make
candle flames flicker and blow out.

Start a new project and delete the cat. Then...

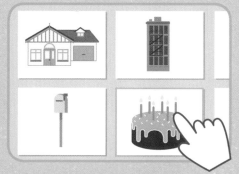

1. Open the character list and find the cake. Tap it once, then tap the paintbrush to get the painting screen.

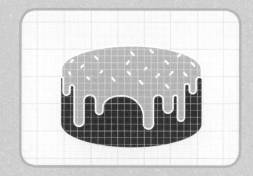

2. You need the candle flames to be separate. So tap the scissor tool and then each lit candle, to remove them.

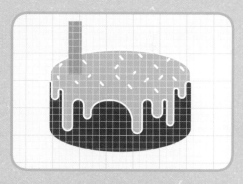

3. Pick a color. Use the rectangle tool to draw a new candle *without* a flame. Use the fill tool to fill it.

4. You can use the copy tool to make more candles, and drag to arrange them. Tap the blue check mark to finish.

I love cake!

LIGHT THE CANDLES

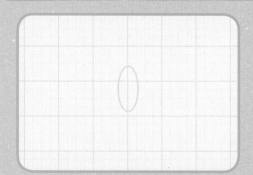

1. Open the character list. Tap the empty box and then the paintbrush. Pick a color and use the oval tool to draw a flame shape. Fill it in.

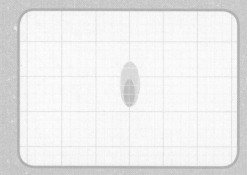

2. Pick a darker color and add a smaller oval on top, like this. Tap the check mark to finish. Now you have one flame character.

You can use a 'grow' block to make the cake bigger.

3. Open the character list. Your flame will appear at the top. Add flames, until you have one for each candle. Drag them into place.

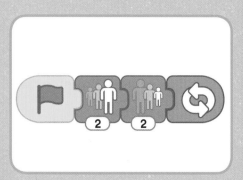

4. Tap the first flame in the list by the stage. Then build this script, using 'grow' and 'shrink' to make it flicker.

'Hide' block

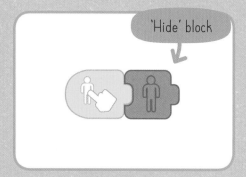

5. Build a second script like this. Now if you touch the flame on stage, it will vanish – as if you have blown it out.

If you have more than four characters, slide your finger up and down this line to see them all.

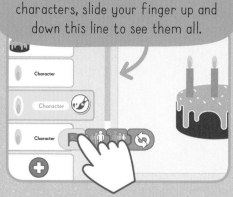

6. Drag both scripts to each of the other flames in the list by the stage, to copy them across.

ADD A GREETING

Tap here to change letter size.

Tap here to change color.

Tap a flame to blow it out

1. To add a greeting, tap the ABC above the stage. This brings up a box where you can type: 'Happy Birthday!'

2. Tap the paint can to pick a color, then tap outside the box to see the text on the stage. Drag it into place.

3. Tap the ABC again, and type: 'Tap a flame to blow it out'. Tap a small 'A' to make the text small. Then tap outside the box and drag the text into place.

ADD MUSIC

Type the number of repeats you want here.

1. Tap the little picture of the cake beside the stage. Go to the 'sounds' menu and record some birthday music.

2. Give the cake this script, to make the music play in a loop with a fixed number of repeats.

Now test your code! Tap the full screen button and the green flag, then try blowing out the candles.

29

PET MONSTER

This project uses **messages** to make a monster do things when you touch different things on screen.

Start a new project and delete the cat. Then...

CHOOSE A MONSTER

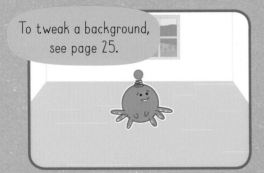

To tweak a background, see page 25.

1. Start by choosing a character to be your pet monster. We used 'Toc', and added the background, 'Empty room'.

Tap the box and type in: That tickles!

1 1 4 That

2. Give the monster this script, to make it ticklish. (The purple 'say' block creates a speech bubble.)

That tickles!

3. Now touch the monster on the stage. It should jiggle and say, 'That tickles!'

MESSAGES

You will need to add another character for each extra thing the monster does. And to make the monster react to the other characters, you'll need messages.

Messages are a way of joining up different pieces of code.

One script sends out a message.

Another script receives the message, and starts to play.

MAKE IT PLAY

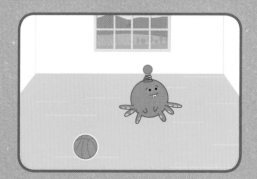

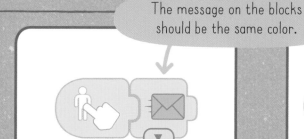
The message on the blocks should be the same color.

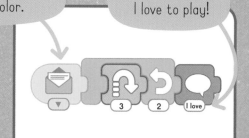
Tap and type in: I love to play!

1. To make the monster play, add a play character. We chose 'Ball'. Drag it into place.

2. Give the ball this script, so it will send out a message when you touch it.

3. Now give the monster this script, so it will react to the message from the ball.

4. Test the code by tapping the ball. Your monster should jump up and down and say, 'I love to play!'

I love to play!

I love to play too!

31

MAKE IT SLEEP

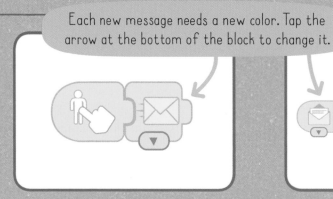

Each new message needs a new color. Tap the arrow at the bottom of the block to change it.

Record a snoring sound.

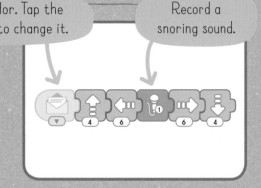

1. To make the monster sleep, add a sleep character. We chose 'Bed'. Drag it into the corner, like this.

2. Give the bed this script, so it sends a message when you touch it. Change the color of the message.

3. Now give the monster this script, so it will react to the message from the bed.

4. Try tapping the bed. Your monster should move to the bed, snore, then go back to the middle.

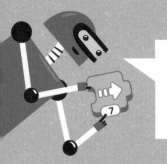

If your monster doesn't end up in the right place, try tweaking the 'move' block numbers.

When characters overlap, the last character you dragged goes in front. So, if your monster vanished behind the bed, drag the monster a little and it'll stay on top.

Sweet dreams!

MAKE IT EAT

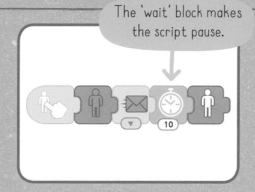

The 'wait' block makes the script pause.

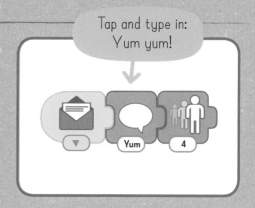

Tap and type in: Yum yum!

1. To make the monster eat, add a food character. We chose 'Apple'. Drag it into place.

2. Give the food this script so that when you touch it, it disappears temporarily and sends a message.

3. Now give the monster this script, so it will react to the message from the food.

4. Tap the food. Your monster should say 'Yum yum' and grow bigger. The food should vanish as if eaten, then reappear.

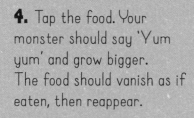

Mmm...

Yum yum!

CAN YOU THINK OF ANY MORE TRICKS TO TEACH YOUR MONSTER?

FAIRY GARDEN

Discover how to add extra backgrounds and switch between them, to create a magical garden.

POP!

Start a new project and delete the cat. Then...

OPENING SCENE

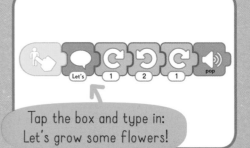

Tap the box and type in: Let's grow some flowers!

1. Tap the background button above the stage and select your opening background. We chose 'Spring'.

2. Add a magical character – we chose 'Fairy' – and drag to arrange it.

3. Give the fairy this script, so she speaks, moves and makes a 'pop' when tapped.

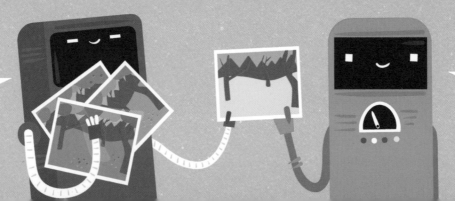

Switching backgrounds is an easy way to make things appear or disappear.

You can have up to four backgrounds in one project.

34

ADD A NEW COPY OF THE BACKGROUND...

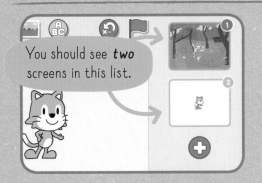

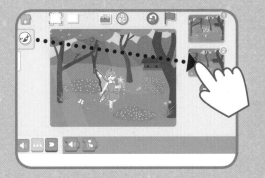

1. To add another background, tap the plus to the right of the stage. The new background will be empty, except for the cat. Delete the cat.

2. Tap the background button and select 'Spring' again. Then tap the first screen in the list to go back. Drag the fairy from the character list...

3. ...to the second screen, to copy her across (along with any scripts). Tap the second screen – the fairy should appear in just the same place.

...AND FILL IT WITH FLOWERS

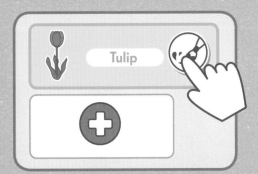

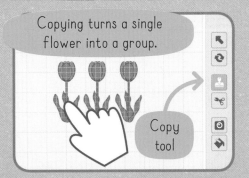

4. Still on the second screen, add a flower character. Then tap the paintbrush, to see the flower in the painting screen.

5. Tap the copy tool and then the flower, and a copy will appear on top of the original. Make a few copies and drag to arrange them. Then tap the check mark.

6. Add a few more, different flower characters in the same way, to fill the garden with blooms. Arrange them by dragging.

MAKE THE SWITCH

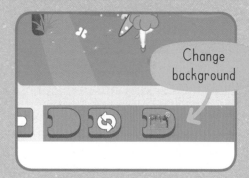

Change background

Numbers help to keep track of which background is which.

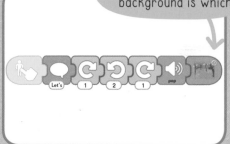

1. Tap the first screen to go back to your original background. Open the red control menu. You should see a new 'change background' block.

2. Add the 'change background' block to the end of the fairy's script. Test it. After the 'pop', the background should switch to the flowery one.

INSTRUCTIONS

Tap the fairy!

Tap here to change letter size.

Tap here to change color.

If you want to tweak the text again, just tap on it.

Tap the fairy!

1. To add instructions, go to the first screen and tap the ABC above the stage. This brings up a box where you can type: 'Tap the fairy!'

2. Tap on the paint can and make the text blue. Then tap outside the box and the text will appear on stage. Drag it into place.

MAKE A BUTTERFLY FLUTTER BY

There are now *three* screens in the list.

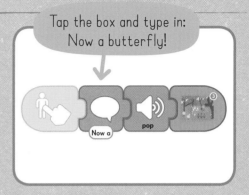

Tap the box and type in: Now a butterfly!

1. For a last touch of magic, tap the plus to add a *third* version of the background. Delete the cat, tap the background button and select 'Spring' again.

2. Tap the second screen in the list to go back. Then drag all the characters over to the third screen, so they appear there too.

3. Still on the second screen, tap the fairy. Drag the old script up to delete it, and replace it with this. Add an instruction: 'Tap again...' in the background.

The green flag will start the script as soon as the background comes up.

4. Tap on the third screen. Then add a butterfly character with this script. Test it – you should see the butterfly flutter back and forth.

SPACE FLIER

Put your new coding skills to use
by creating this space game.

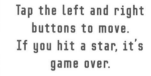

The aim of this game
is to keep your
rocket dodging
between the stars.

Tap the left and right
buttons to move.
If you hit a star, it's
game over.

Start a new project and delete the cat. Then...

SET THE SCENE

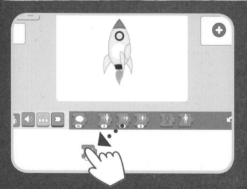

We made the stars yellow
so they're easier to see.

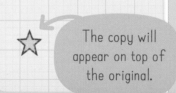

The copy will
appear on top of
the original.

Don't add too many stars, and
make sure you leave gaps.

1. Start by adding a space rocket. Get a purple 'shrink' block and tap it a few times to make the rocket smaller. Then, add a star.

2. Find the star in the list beside the stage, and tap the paintbrush for the painting screen. Tap the copy tool and then the star, to make a copy.

3. Drag the stars apart. Add a few more copies the same way. Spread them out, then tap the check mark. Your character is now a *group* of stars.

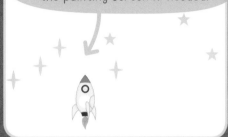

Leave a gap just above the rocket. You can tweak your star groups in the painting screen if needed.

4. Repeat with a different star, so you have two groups. Drag the star groups and rocket to arrange them like this on the stage.

5. Tap the background button above the stage. Tap a background to select it – we chose 'Space'. Tap again to see it on the stage.

Dodge the stars!

6. Tap the ABC above the stage and type in some instructions: 'Dodge the stars!' Tap the paint can and make the text yellow.

MOVING STARS

1. Create this script for the first star group. Then tap the green flag above the stage. The group should keep moving down in an endless loop.

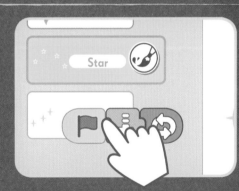

Star

2. Tap and drag the script to the second star group, to copy it across. Now if you tap the green flag, *all* the stars should move.

When the stars move, the rocket seems to fly.

ROCKET CONTROLS

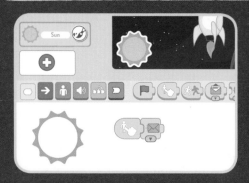

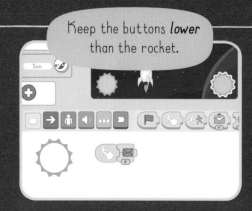

Keep the buttons *lower* than the rocket.

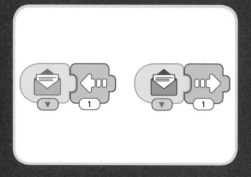

1. Add a character on the left, to use as a left button (we chose 'Sun'). Then give it this script.

2. Add another character on the right, to use as a right button, and give it this script.

3. Now give the rocket these two scripts, so it will move left or right if the buttons are tapped.

ADD A GAME OVER SCREEN

There are now two screens in this list.

1. Tap the plus sign to the right of the stage, to add a second background. It will start out white with the cat again. Delete the cat.

2. Use the background button to add the same background as before. Add some text for when the game is over: 'Oh no, you hit it!'

3. Tap the first background in the list, and create this script for the rocket. Now, if it bumps another character (any of the stars), the background will switch to the game over screen.

TESTING, TESTING

Tap the full-screen button and try playing. How long can you keep going?

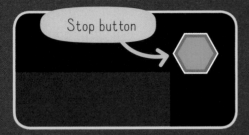

If you want to tweak the position of anything, tap the red stop button. Then go back to the coding screen and drag to rearrange things.

To reset the game so you can play again, go to the coding screen and tap the little start screen on the right of the stage.

PLAY AGAIN

Adding this makes it easier to play again.

1. Go to the game over screen and add a single star. Use a 'grow' block to make it bigger. Then add some text: 'Tap the star to play again.'

2. Tap the star and create this code. Now, when you touch the star, it will take you back to the first screen, so you can keep playing.

HANDY TIPS

Here are some useful extra tips –
including what to do if things go wrong.

NAMING PROJECTS

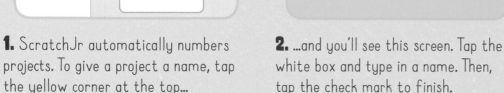

1. ScratchJr automatically numbers projects. To give a project a name, tap the yellow corner at the top...

2. ...and you'll see this screen. Tap the white box and type in a name. Then, tap the check mark to finish.

3. Tap the house to go to the project page. The name you typed will now appear below the picture of your project.

EXTRA HELP

To watch an introduction to ScratchJr, or explore sample projects, tap the question mark at the top of the screen.

When you want to go back to the project page, just tap the house.

Tap here to play the introduction.

If you're unsure what a block in the menu does, tap and hold it – and a blue label will pop up, like this.

Ooooh!

TROUBLESHOOTING

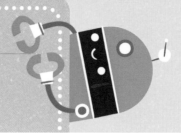

IF STRANGE THINGS HAPPEN WHEN YOU TOUCH THE SCREEN

- Make sure you're not leaning on the screen.
- Use only one finger to tap.
- Make sure the screen and your fingers are clean; dirt can confuse the touch sensors.

IF YOUR CODE DOESN'T DO WHAT YOU EXPECTED

You've found what coders call a **bug**. Don't worry, it happens to everyone! First, think about what's going wrong. Which script controls that part? Then, look at that script to see if you can spot something wrong. If you can't, ask someone else to try. A fresh pair of eyes can help.

IF YOUR PROJECT SUDDENLY STOPS WORKING

Something may have gone wrong inside the ScratchJr app, making it **crash** or stop working. Try closing the app (see below) and restarting it. If that doesn't work, ask a grown-up to turn the tablet off and on again.

Pssst... on an iPad®, press the home button to close the window. Then double press the home button to see a list of all the apps running. Find the ScratchJr icon and drag it upwards to close it completely.

GOING FURTHER

If you enjoy ScratchJr but are ready to do more, you may like to try coding with Scratch. Scratch is similar to ScratchJr, but has more blocks – and more things you can do with them. It is also free. Go to

www.usborne.com/quicklinks

for more information and links.

BLOCK LIST

Here are all the blocks in ScratchJr and what they do.

TRIGGER BLOCKS

 START ON GREEN FLAG
Makes a script start when you tap the green flag above the stage.

 START ON TAP
Makes a script start when you tap a character.

 START ON BUMP
Makes a script start when one character is bumped by another.

 START ON MESSAGE
Makes a script start when it receives a message of a certain color.

Tap here to select the color.

 SEND MESSAGE
Sends a message of a certain color.

MOTION BLOCKS

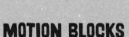 **MOVE RIGHT**
Moves a character to the right.

Tap here to set how far it moves.

 MOVE LEFT
Moves a character to the left.

 MOVE UP
Moves a character up.

 MOVE DOWN
Moves a character down.

 TURN RIGHT
Turns a character clockwise.

Tap here to set how much to turn. Type in 12 for a complete turn.

 TURN LEFT
Turns a character counter-clockwise.

 HOP
Moves a character up and down again.

 GO HOME
Makes a character go back to where it started.

LOOKS BLOCKS

 SAY
Gives a character a speech bubble with a message.

Tap here to type in the message.

 GROW
Makes a character bigger.

Tap here to set how much bigger.

 SHRINK
Makes a character smaller.

 RESET SIZE
Makes a character go back to its normal size.

 HIDE
Makes a character fade and disappear.

 SHOW
Makes a character reappear.

SOUND BLOCKS

 **POP**
Plays a 'pop'.

 PLAY RECORDED SOUND
Allows you to record and play your own sound.

CONTROL BLOCKS

 WAIT
Makes a script wait for a set amount of time.

Tap here to set how long.

 STOP
Makes all of a character's scripts stop.

 SET SPEED
Changes the speed at which some blocks run.

Tap here to select the speed.

REPEAT

 Makes the blocks inside it repeat a certain number of times.

Tap here to set the number of times.

END BLOCKS

 END
This doesn't 'do' anything, but can be added to mark the end of a script.

 REPEAT FOREVER
Makes a script keep repeating.

NOTES FOR GROWN-UPS

As well as coding, there are lots of other things children can do on a tablet –
but please be aware they can also access material that is not suitable for them.

FUN AND GAMES

Tablets usually come with apps to play music and videos, but these are just players – you need to add the actual music and videos yourself. You can also add games, but check age recommendations carefully first. Beware of games which may include inappropriate advertising, or encourage spending through in-app purchases.

> The easiest way to add music, movies or games is to download them from an online store.
> This usually costs money, but you can find links to some fun, FREE games and activities at:
> **www.usborne.com/quicklinks**

Set up your tablet to ask for your password or check your id before allowing new downloads, and turn off in-app purchases.*

SCREEN TIME

'Screen time' means time spent watching TV, or using a smartphone, tablet or other computer. Whenever possible, share screen time with your child, chatting about what they are doing or watching. It's not healthy for anyone, especially young children, to spend a long time in front of a screen – so monitor screen time and set limits.

> Experts recommend children aged 2-5 have no more than 1 hour of screen time per day, and older children maintain a mix of activities.

For older children, consider installing a timer that turns the tablet off automatically after a certain time.*

*For more advice and instructions, go to: www.usborne.com/quicklinks

USING THE INTERNET

The internet is a great resource, with websites for everything from games and videos to homework help. But it is important children learn how to use it safely.

Young children should *always* be supervised while using the internet. With older children, talk to them about internet safety and make sure they know when to ask for help. Children under 13 should not use social media sites such as Facebook or Instagram.

Set parental controls on your tablet* to help filter out unsuitable content, but don't rely on them to catch everything. When searching for websites, it's a good idea to include 'kids' or 'children' in your search terms. This should help to make the results more child-friendly.

You can find examples of fun, child-friendly websites to explore by visiting:

www.usborne.com/ quicklinks

and entering the keywords: 'scratch jr'.

STAYING SAFE

The internet is a public space and it's very easy for children to stumble across things that are not suitable for them. Teach children the basic safety rules: ask a grown-up before going online and, if they are asked to give information about themselves, send a photo or come across *anything* they're not sure about, stop and tell a grown-up.

Please follow the internet safety guidelines at:

www.usborne.com/ quicklinks

TURNING IT OFF

For young children, you can quickly turn off internet access by putting the tablet into airplane mode (also known as flight mode) without wifi.*

A wifi symbol at the top of the screen means the tablet is connected to the internet.

An airplane symbol at the top shows the tablet is in airplane mode.

INDEX

Thanks to Bella Woodhall, age 7, for testing the projects. American editor: Carrie Armstrong.

First published in 2018 by Usborne Publishing Ltd., Usborne House, 83-85 Saffron Hill, London, EC1N 8RT, United Kingdom.

www.usborne.com

Photos on p.28 courtesy Rosie Dickins.
iPad is a trademark of Apple Inc., registered in the U.S. and other countries.
Fire and all related logos are trademarks of Amazon.com, Inc. or its affiliates.
iOS is a trademark or registered trademark of Cisco in the U.S. and other countries and is used under license.
Android is a trademark of Google LLC.